I0013091

Nikon Z5II User Guide

Step-by-Step Instructions for Capturing
Stunning Photos and Videos, Plus
Expert Tips for Advanced Techniques
& Settings

Oksana Chalifour

1

Disclaimer

The information provided in this book is intended to help users better understand and make the most of the Nikon Z5II camera. While every effort has been made to ensure accuracy and clarity, the author does not claim to be affiliated with Nikon Corporation. This book is an independent guide, and all brand names, logos, and trademarks mentioned are the property of their respective owners.

The content, tips, and advice in this book are based on the author's research and personal experience. The reader is encouraged to consult the official Nikon manual and website for the latest updates, firmware releases, and additional technical support.

This book is not intended to replace official documentation or expert training. The author and publisher are not liable for any damage, loss, or injury resulting from the use of the information provided herein.

Table Of Contents

Introduction

The **Nikon Z5II** is a versatile and powerful mirrorless camera that offers exceptional image quality, advanced features, and ease of use. Whether you are a photography enthusiast stepping up your game, a vlogger creating high-quality videos, or a seasoned photographer looking for a reliable second camera, the Z5II delivers everything you need to capture stunning shots and videos with ease.

What sets the Z5II apart from other cameras in its class is its **full-frame sensor, exceptional autofocus performance**, and robust video capabilities. It's perfect for those looking to expand their creative possibilities, with the ability to handle a wide variety of subjects, environments, and shooting styles.

Who the Nikon Z5II is For

The **Nikon Z5II** is designed for:

- **Beginner and intermediate photographers** looking for a full-frame camera with easy-to-use features.

- **Vloggers and content creators** who need a camera that delivers both stunning stills and high-quality videos.

- **Travel and landscape photographers** who need a durable, portable, and capable camera for all conditions.

- **Professional photographers** who want a secondary camera or something lighter than their primary setup without compromising on image quality.

No matter your skill level, the Z5II is intuitive enough for newcomers while still offering advanced features for more experienced users.

Key Features and Highlights

- **Full-Frame CMOS Sensor**: Capture detailed, rich images with stunning dynamic range and depth of field.

- **Advanced Hybrid Autofocus**: With 273 AF points, including Eye-Detection and Animal-Detection, the Z5II's autofocus is fast and reliable.

- **4K Video Recording**: The Z5II shoots 4K UHD video at up to 30 fps, making it ideal for creators looking to make cinematic content.

- **In-Body Image Stabilization (IBIS)**: Reduce shake and achieve clearer, sharper shots, even in low-light or handheld situations.

- **Dual SD Card Slots**: Save your photos and videos on two memory cards simultaneously for redundancy and peace of mind.

- **Built-In Wi-Fi and Bluetooth**: Easily transfer images, control your camera remotely, and streamline your workflow with Nikon's mobile app integration.

- **Weather-Sealed Body**: Designed to withstand challenging conditions, perfect for outdoor shooting.

These features make the Z5II an all-around powerhouse that excels in both still photography and video production, perfect for versatile creators.

Unboxing the Z5II

What's in the Box

Camera Body Overview

Once you open the box, the **Nikon Z5II body** is neatly secured and ready to go. The body is compact but sturdy, featuring a comfortable grip with a robust design that feels balanced in your hands. The camera is designed for ease of use, with buttons and dials placed for intuitive access while shooting.

- **Front View**: Includes the lens mount, the autofocus sensor, and the Z-mount.

- **Top View**: Features the shutter button, mode dial, and a top LCD screen.

- **Back View**: Equipped with a vari-angle touchscreen for easy navigation and a viewfinder.

- **Right Side**: Memory card slots and USB-C/HDMI ports.

- **Left Side**: Battery compartment with access to the microphone and headphone ports.

Lens Kit Options

The Z5II is often sold with a **Nikkor Z 24-50mm f/4-6.3 lens** kit, which is versatile for general photography. This lens is compact and covers a standard zoom range, making it perfect for daily photography needs, from wide-angle landscapes to moderate telephoto shots.

If you prefer, you can also buy the camera body without the lens and select your own lens depending on your needs. Popular choices include:

- **Nikkor Z 50mm f/1.8 S**: Great for portraits and low-light situations.

- **Nikkor Z 24-70mm f/2.8 S**: Ideal for professional-quality shots in various focal lengths.

Included Accessories

When unboxing the Z5II, you'll find the following accessories:

- **EN-EL15C Rechargeable Battery**: Provides ample power for your shoots.

- **MH-25A Battery Charger**: Charges the camera battery. You can also charge the camera via USB-C if you're on the go.

- **Strap**: Standard camera strap to keep your camera secure while carrying it around.

- **USB-C Cable**: For charging and transferring files.

- **Body Cap**: Protects the camera from dust and debris when not in use.

- **User Manual**: A detailed guide on using the Z5II, but you'll likely refer to this step-by-step guide for more clarity!

Recommended Optional Gear

To enhance your Z5II experience, consider investing in the following:

- **Extra Batteries**: So you're never caught without power during long shoots.

- **High-Speed SD Cards**: To take full advantage of the Z5II's features like 4K video recording and high-speed burst shooting.

- **Tripod**: For long exposures and steady video work.

- **External Microphone**: For better sound quality, especially for video creators.

- **ND Filters**: Help manage exposure when shooting in bright conditions, especially for video.

- **Protective Case**: To keep your gear safe when traveling.

Camera Body Design and Ergonomics

The **Nikon Z5II** is designed to offer a comfortable and secure grip, making it suitable for extended shooting sessions. The button layout is intuitive, and the camera body itself feels solid but lightweight for its size. You'll appreciate the **weather-sealed design**, which gives you the confidence to shoot in less-than-ideal conditions, whether it's dusty, rainy, or snowy.

The **rotatable LCD touchscreen** makes shooting at unusual angles, such as low or high perspectives, simple. Additionally, the **electronic viewfinder** allows you to see your scene exactly as the sensor captures it, ensuring accurate framing and exposure even in bright sunlight.

Lens Kit Options

As mentioned, the **Nikkor Z 24-50mm f/4-6.3 lens** is the most common kit option, but it's important to know that the Z5II supports a wide range of **Z-mount lenses**. These lenses offer fantastic image quality and seamless autofocus. When choosing lenses, think about the subjects you most frequently shoot:

- **Portraits**: Consider fast prime lenses like the **Nikkor Z 85mm f/1.8 S**.

- **Landscapes**: A wide-angle lens like the **Nikkor Z 14-30mm f/4 S** can capture expansive scenes with sharp detail.

- **Wildlife and Sports**: A telephoto zoom lens like the **Nikkor Z 70-200mm f/2.8 VR S** is a great choice.

Recommended Memory Cards

To get the best performance out of the Z5II, use **UHS-II SD cards**, as they support fast read/write speeds, ideal for 4K video and continuous shooting. Popular options include:

- **SanDisk Extreme Pro 64GB UHS-II**

- **Lexar Professional 1000x 64GB UHS-II**

You can use **UHS-I cards** in the Z5II, but they won't be as fast for video or burst photography.

By following these steps and tips, you'll be well on your way to mastering the Nikon Z5II, from unboxing to shooting like a pro. The Z5II is packed with features that empower you to take your photography and videography to the next level—whether you're capturing a breathtaking landscape or creating cinematic video content.

Setting Up Your Nikon Z5II

Congratulations on choosing the Nikon Z5II! Let's get your camera set up properly so you can start shooting in no time. This guide will walk you through every step of the setup process, with clear, detailed instructions to help you understand each action and make the most out of your camera.

Understanding the Z5II Layout

Before we dive into the setup process, let's get familiar with the camera's layout. Knowing where everything is will make your setup and shooting experience more intuitive.

Front, Top, and Rear View

- **Front**: This is where you'll find the Nikon Z-mount for attaching your lenses. There's also a grip that fits comfortably in your hand.

- **Top**: The top panel houses the mode dial, which lets you select different shooting modes. There's also the shutter button, the power switch, and the microphone port.

- **Rear**: Here, you'll see the LCD touchscreen display, buttons for navigating menus, and the joystick for focus point control. The viewfinder is located here too.

Button, Dial, and Touchscreen Functions

- **Mode Dial**: Switch between different shooting modes, such as Auto, Manual (M), Aperture Priority (A), Shutter Priority (S), and others.

- **Menu Button**: Use this to access the camera's settings and change preferences.

- **Joystick**: This helps you select your autofocus points easily.

- **Touchscreen**: Tap to focus or navigate through menus and settings.

Ports, Connectors, and Slots Explained

- **USB-C Port**: For charging your camera and transferring files.

- **HDMI Port**: For connecting the camera to an external monitor or TV.

- **Memory Card Slots**: The Z5II has two SD card slots for extended storage. We'll go into how to use them shortly.

Preparing Your Camera

Now that you're familiar with the camera's layout, let's begin setting it up.

Installing the Battery and Dual SD Cards

1. **Open the Battery Compartment**: Slide the latch at the bottom of the camera to open the battery compartment.

2. **Insert the Battery**: Take the battery and line it up with the compartment's connectors. Slide it in until it clicks into place.

19

3. **Insert Your SD Cards**: The Z5II uses two SD cards. Insert your first card into Slot 1 (on the right side) and the second into Slot 2. The camera can handle two different modes for these cards, such as overflow or backup. We'll explain that soon.

4. **Close the Compartment**: Once both the battery and cards are in place, close the compartment and ensure it locks securely.

First-Time Charging (USB-C and Wall Charger)

- **Via USB-C**: Plug the provided USB-C cable into the USB-C port of the camera. Connect the other end to a power source, such as a laptop or a USB wall adapter.

- **Via Wall Charger**: You can also charge the battery separately using the wall charger. Insert the battery into the charger, then plug the charger into a wall outlet.

Inserting and Formatting Memory Cards

1. **Insert the SD Cards**: Insert your SD card into the card slot as we discussed earlier.

2. **Formatting**: Turn on your camera. Go to the **Menu > Setup Menu > Format Card**. Select your card and confirm. This will erase any data on the card and prepare it for use with the camera.

Recommended Memory Cards (UHS-I vs UHS-II)

- **UHS-I Cards**: These are standard SD cards and are perfect for general photography.

- **UHS-II Cards**: These offer faster read and write speeds, which is beneficial if you plan on shooting high-quality 4K video or burst-mode photography.

Attaching and Detaching Lenses

Now let's move on to the lens. It's important to attach and detach your lenses properly to avoid damaging the camera or lens.

Mounting Z-Mount Lenses

1. **Align the Lens and Camera Mount**: Take the lens and line up the red dot on the lens with the red dot on the camera's lens mount.

2. **Attach the Lens**: Gently push the lens into the mount and turn it clockwise until you hear a click, which means the lens is securely attached.

3. **Check for Lock**: Make sure the lens is fully locked in place before you start shooting.

Using F-Mount Lenses (with FTZ Adapter)

If you're using older Nikon lenses with an F-mount, you'll need the FTZ (F to Z) adapter.

1. **Attach the FTZ Adapter**: First, attach the FTZ adapter to the camera's Z-mount.

2. **Mount the F-Mount Lens**: Then, attach your F-mount lens to the FTZ adapter just like you would with a Z-mount lens.

Sensor Protection and Dust Prevention Tips

- **Keep the Lens Mounted**: When not using the camera, always keep a lens mounted to protect the sensor from dust and debris.

- **Use the Body Cap**: When not using the camera at all, attach the body cap to cover the sensor.

Essential First Settings

Let's now move on to configuring your camera's settings for the best experience.

Language, Date, and Time

1. Turn on your camera by switching the power button.

2. The camera will prompt you to select your language. Use the touchscreen or joystick to select your preferred language.

3. Set the date and time by using the same method. This is crucial for accurate timestamps on your photos and videos.

Image Quality Settings (RAW vs JPEG)

1. Press the **Menu** button.

2. Go to the **Photo Shooting Menu**.

3. Select **Image Quality**.

4. Choose between **RAW** (high-quality, large files) or **JPEG** (smaller files, easier to store and share). If you're a beginner, JPEG is fine for everyday use, but RAW gives you more editing control.

Setting Up Auto Backup on Dual Cards

1. In the **Menu**, go to **Setup Menu** > **Card Slot Settings**.

2. Choose **Backup** for both cards. This ensures that photos are saved on both cards at the same time, providing extra security in case one card fails.

Checking and Updating Firmware

1. Go to the **Menu** > **Setup Menu** > **Firmware Version**.

2. Check the current firmware version of your camera.

3. To update, visit Nikon's website on your computer, find the latest firmware for the Z5II, and follow the instructions to download and install it.

Final Checks and Ready to Shoot

With your camera set up, it's time to take a final check to ensure everything is in order:

- Confirm that the battery is fully charged.

- Ensure your memory cards are correctly formatted and ready to use.

- Verify that the lens is securely attached.

- Go through the menu once more to ensure your settings are exactly how you want them.

Congratulations, you've successfully set up your Nikon Z5II! Now you're ready to start capturing stunning photos and videos. Remember, the Z5II is packed with advanced features, but don't hesitate to revisit this guide as you explore more about the camera's full capabilities.

Enjoy your photography journey with the Nikon Z5II, and remember that every great photographer starts with a single step—this setup process!

Understanding Camera Basics

What Is a Full-Frame Camera?

A **full-frame camera** is a type of digital camera that uses a sensor the size of a **35mm film frame**. Think of it as a more advanced version of older film cameras, but with a digital twist. A **larger sensor** allows more light and more details in your photos.

Why Does Full-Frame Matter?

1. **Better Image Quality**: The full-frame sensor captures more light, meaning your photos will be **clearer**, with **better colors** and **less grainy** noise, especially in low light.

2. **Wider Field of View**: A full-frame camera captures more of a scene, which is great for landscape shots or group photos.

3. **Shallow Depth of Field**: Full-frame cameras allow you to create beautiful **blurred backgrounds**, perfect for portraits.

Full-Frame vs. Crop Sensor: What's the Difference?

Full-Frame Camera

- Larger sensor.

- Captures more light and detail.

- Offers a wider view and better low-light performance.

Crop Sensor Camera

- Smaller sensor, meaning less light and detail.

- Crops your image, which makes distant subjects appear closer (like zooming in).

- Works well for some situations but doesn't perform as well in low light.

Mastering Exposure Basics

Exposure refers to how much light is allowed to reach your camera's sensor. A good exposure means your photo is neither too bright nor too dark. You control exposure with **three main settings**: **Shutter Speed**, **Aperture**, and **ISO**.

Shutter Speed

Shutter speed controls how fast or slow the camera's shutter opens and closes. It affects how motion is captured in your photos.

- **Fast Shutter Speed** (e.g., 1/1000): Freezes fast-moving subjects.

- **Slow Shutter Speed** (e.g., 1/30): Captures motion blur, such as flowing water.

How to Adjust on the Nikon Z5II:

1. Turn the mode dial to **S** (Shutter Priority).

2. Use the **front dial** to adjust the shutter speed.

3. The camera will automatically adjust the aperture.

Aperture (F-Stop)

Aperture is the opening in your lens that controls how much light passes through to the sensor. It's measured in **f-stops** (like f/1.8, f/5.6).

- **Small f-stop (e.g., f/1.8)**: Lets in more light and creates a **blurry background** (great for portraits).

- **Large f-stop (e.g., f/16)**: Lets in less light and keeps more of the scene in **focus** (great for landscapes).

How to Adjust on the Nikon Z5II:

1. Turn the mode dial to **A** (Aperture Priority).

2. Use the **rear dial** to adjust the aperture (f-stop).

3. The camera will adjust the shutter speed automatically.

ISO Sensitivity

ISO controls how sensitive the camera's sensor is to light. A higher ISO means your camera can shoot in darker conditions, but it may also introduce **grainy noise**.

- **Low ISO (100-400)**: Best for bright settings, like daytime outdoors.

- **High ISO (1600-3200)**: Useful for low-light situations but may cause some grain.

How to Adjust on the Nikon Z5II:

1. Press the **ISO button** on the top of the camera.

2. Use the **rear dial** to adjust the ISO value.

Exploring Shooting Modes

The Nikon Z5II has several modes that allow you to control how much the camera does for you and how much you control. Let's break down each mode.

Auto Mode (Green Auto Icon)

In **Auto Mode**, the camera handles everything automatically, including shutter speed, aperture, and ISO. This is ideal for beginners who want to focus just on **composition**.

How to Use:

1. Turn the mode dial to the **green Auto symbol**.

2. Point and shoot. The camera will take care of the settings for you.

When to Use: When you want quick, simple shots without worrying about settings.

Program Mode (P)

In **Program Mode**, the camera chooses shutter speed and aperture, but you can adjust other settings like ISO, white balance, and flash.

How to Use:

1. Turn the mode dial to **P**.

2. Use the **rear dial** to adjust settings like ISO or white balance.

3. The camera sets the shutter speed and aperture for proper exposure.

When to Use: When you want more control but still want the camera to do some of the work.

Shutter Priority Mode (S)

In **Shutter Priority Mode**, you control the shutter speed, and the camera adjusts the aperture.

How to Use:

1. Turn the mode dial to **S**.

2. Use the **front dial** to adjust the shutter speed.

3. The camera will automatically set the aperture for you.

When to Use: To freeze fast-moving subjects (e.g., sports) or create motion blur effects.

Aperture Priority Mode (A)

In **Aperture Priority Mode**, you control the aperture (f-stop), and the camera adjusts the shutter speed.

How to Use:

1. Turn the mode dial to **A**.

2. Use the **rear dial** to adjust the f-stop.

3. The camera adjusts the shutter speed accordingly.

When to Use: To control depth of field, such as blurring the background in portraits.

Manual Mode (M)

In **Manual Mode**, you have complete control over both shutter speed and aperture.

How to Use:

1. Turn the mode dial to **M**.

2. Use the **front dial** to adjust the shutter speed.

3. Use the **rear dial** to adjust the aperture.

4. Set the **ISO** manually by pressing the **ISO button**.

When to Use: For full creative control, or when shooting in tricky lighting situations.

Scene Modes & Creative Effects

Scene Modes adjust the camera settings automatically for specific situations, like portraits or landscapes.

- **Portrait Mode**: Optimizes settings for a blurred background (great for portraits).

- **Landscape Mode**: Keeps everything in focus with a small aperture (good for wide landscapes).

Creative Effects add artistic touches, like the **Miniature Effect** or **Selective Color**.

Mastering the Menu and Touchscreen

The Nikon Z5II has a simple, intuitive menu system and touchscreen that lets you access settings quickly.

Navigating Menus Quickly

1. Press the **Menu** button to open the main menu.

2. Use the **directional pad** or **touchscreen** to scroll through options.

3. To select an option, press the **OK button**.

Customizing the "i" Menu and My Menu

1. **i-Menu**: This menu gives you quick access to frequently used settings.

   o Press the **i-button** on the back of the camera.

   o Customize the settings you want to show up by going to **Menu > Custom Settings > Customize i-Menu**.

2. **My Menu**: Personalize a menu for your favorite settings.

   o Go to **Menu > Custom Settings > My Menu**.

   o Press **Add Item** to add settings like **White Balance** or **Focus Mode**.

By now, you should feel comfortable with your Nikon Z5II, understanding the basics of exposure and how to use various shooting modes. You've also learned how to navigate the camera's menu and touchscreen quickly, customizing it to your preferences. With practice, you'll be able to create beautiful photos and videos while gaining more creative control over your shots.

Mastering Focus, Exposure, and Stabilization

Welcome to your hands-on workshop for mastering focus, exposure, and image stabilization with your Nikon Z5II! This guide will break down every essential aspect of the camera's focus system, metering, and stabilization, all in a way that's easy to understand and follow, especially for beginners. No shortcuts — just clear, actionable steps to help you get the most out of your camera.

Autofocus Modes Explained: AF-S, AF-C, AF-A

The Nikon Z5II uses **Autofocus (AF)** to lock onto your subject and keep it sharp. The Z5II has three main autofocus modes to help you in different shooting scenarios.

AF-S (Autofocus Single)

- **When to Use It**: Use AF-S when you're photographing stationary subjects or when you have time to focus.

- **How it Works**: In this mode, the camera focuses once when you press the shutter halfway, and it locks the focus until you release the shutter button. It's perfect for portraits, still life, or landscape shots.

Step-by-Step:

1. Turn the mode dial on the camera to **AF-S**.

2. Half-press the shutter button.

3. Wait for the focus confirmation, then fully press the shutter to take the photo.

Practical Example: When taking a portrait, your subject isn't moving, so you want to ensure that their face is sharp. AF-S will allow you to lock focus on the face before capturing the shot.

AF-C (Autofocus Continuous)

- **When to Use It**: AF-C is ideal for tracking moving subjects, such as athletes, animals, or cars.

- **How it Works**: With AF-C, the camera constantly adjusts focus as long as the shutter button is half-pressed. It's great for dynamic scenes where your subject is in motion.

Step-by-Step:

1. Turn the mode dial on the camera to **AF-C**.

2. Half-press the shutter button.

3. The camera will continuously adjust the focus as your subject moves within the frame.

4. Fully press the shutter to capture the image.

Practical Example: If you're shooting a soccer game, the players are moving constantly, so AF-C ensures they remain in focus even when they run across the field.

AF-A (Autofocus Automatic)

- **When to Use It**: AF-A is a hybrid mode that automatically switches between AF-S and AF-C, depending on the subject's movement.

- **How it Works**: If your subject stays still, the camera will use AF-S. If the subject begins to move, the camera will switch to AF-C for continuous focusing.

Step-by-Step:

1. Turn the mode dial on the camera to **AF-A**.

2. The camera will automatically decide whether to use single or continuous autofocus depending on the situation.

3. Half-press the shutter button and wait for focus confirmation before fully pressing to capture the photo.

Practical Example: You're shooting an event with both stationary and moving people, and AF-A will adjust automatically as they move.

Manual Focus Techniques

While autofocus modes are often faster, sometimes you may want to use **manual focus** for precise control, especially in tricky lighting or when capturing small, detailed subjects like insects or macro photography.

How to Use Manual Focus:

1. Set the camera's focus mode switch (on the lens) to **M** (Manual).

2. Turn the **focus ring** on your lens to focus.

3. Use the **focus peaking** feature (if enabled) to see the areas that are in focus. The camera will highlight in-color parts of the image that are sharp.

Tip: Press the **OK button** on the back of the camera to activate focus magnification. This allows you to zoom in and see your subject more clearly, ensuring sharpness.

Subject Detection Autofocus: Face, Eye, Animal, Vehicle

The Nikon Z5II offers advanced **subject detection** technology that can automatically detect faces, eyes, animals, and even vehicles. Here's how you can use these features:

Face Detection

- **When to Use**: Ideal for portraits, the camera will automatically detect and focus on the face of your subject.

How to Use:

1. Go to the **Focus Area** settings in the camera's menu and enable **Face Detection**.

2. When you point the camera at someone, it will automatically find and focus on their face.

Practical Example: When shooting a family portrait, the camera will lock onto your subject's face for perfect focus

Eye Detection (Human/Animal)

- **When to Use**: Eye detection ensures that the eyes of your subject are always in sharp focus —

especially crucial for portraits and animal photography.

How to Use:

1. In the **Auto Focus Mode** settings, select **Eye Detection**.

2. Ensure the camera recognizes the human or animal face.

3. The camera will automatically focus on the nearest eye (human or animal).

Practical Example: For pet photography, Eye Detection helps ensure that the animal's eye is always in sharp focus, even if they're moving.

Vehicle Detection

- **When to Use**: Vehicle detection is useful for motorsport or any scenario where fast-moving vehicles are involved.

How to Use:

1. In the **AF Area Mode**, choose the **Vehicle Detection** option.

2. The camera will track vehicles, ensuring they stay in focus while you capture fast-moving action shots.

Practical Example: At a car race, the camera will track the cars and keep them in focus even as they zoom past.

Focus Area Modes: Choose the Right Focus Zone

The Nikon Z5II gives you several options for selecting how the camera focuses on subjects. Here's a breakdown of each **Focus Area Mode**:

Auto-Area AF

- **When to Use**: Auto-Area AF is perfect when you want the camera to decide where to focus automatically. It's ideal when you need to capture a scene quickly.

How to Use:

1. Set the camera to **Auto-Area AF**.

2. The camera will use the entire frame to detect and focus on any subjects in the scene.

Practical Example: In a group shot, Auto-Area AF will focus on the most prominent subjects in the scene, such as people in the foreground.

Single-Point AF

- **When to Use**: Single-Point AF gives you more control, allowing you to select a specific point in the frame for focus.

How to Use:

1. Set the camera to **Single-Point AF**.

2. Use the **multi-selector** or touchscreen to choose a specific focus point in the viewfinder or on the LCD screen.

Practical Example: When capturing a close-up shot of a flower, you can focus precisely on a single petal.

Dynamic-Area AF

- **When to Use**: Dynamic-Area AF is great for moving subjects. The camera will focus on the selected point but will also track your subject if it moves away from the original focus point.

How to Use:

1. Set the camera to **Dynamic-Area AF**.

2. Select your primary focus point.

3. If the subject moves, the camera will shift focus to follow them.

Practical Example: If you're shooting a dog running, Dynamic-Area AF helps you track them as they move through the frame.

Wide-Area AF

- **When to Use**: Wide-Area AF uses a larger area to focus, ensuring multiple subjects within the area are sharp.

How to Use:

1. Set the camera to **Wide-Area AF**.

2. The camera will focus across a broader area, making it easier to capture scenes with multiple subjects.

Practical Example: If you're photographing a crowd, Wide-Area AF ensures that more people stay in focus, even if they're spread out.

3D-Tracking

- **When to Use**: 3D-Tracking is great for tracking subjects that move unpredictably. The camera tracks the subject's motion and maintains focus on them.

How to Use:

1. Set the camera to **3D-Tracking**.

2. The camera will track your subject even if they move across the frame.

Practical Example: In a basketball game, the camera will track the players as they move across the court in all directions.

Understanding Exposure Metering

The Nikon Z5II has four different metering modes to help you get the perfect exposure for your photos.

Matrix Metering

- **When to Use**: This is the default metering mode. It evaluates the entire scene and determines the best exposure based on various factors like brightness and contrast.

How to Use:

1. Set the camera to **Matrix Metering**.

2. The camera will automatically adjust settings to give you a balanced exposure.

Center-Weighted Metering

- **When to Use**: Use this mode when you want the camera to focus on the center of the image but still consider the rest of the scene.

How to Use:

1. Set the camera to **Center-Weighted Metering**.

2. The camera will prioritize the exposure for the center of the frame.

Spot Metering

- **When to Use**: Use Spot Metering when you need precise control over the exposure of a specific area in the frame, such as a person's face or a small object.

How to Use:

1. Set the camera to **Spot Metering**.

2. The camera will measure exposure based on the small spot you select.

Highlight-Weighted Metering

- **When to Use**: Use Highlight-Weighted Metering to prioritize exposure for bright areas, ensuring that highlights don't get overexposed.

How to Use:

1. Set the camera to **Highlight-Weighted Metering**.

2. The camera will adjust exposure to prevent highlights from clipping.

Using Image Stabilization (IBIS)

IBIS helps reduce camera shake and allows you to shoot at slower shutter speeds without blurring your images. This is especially helpful for handheld photography.

How IBIS Works:

- The **In-Body Image Stabilization** system physically moves the camera's sensor to counteract any camera shake.

- When shooting handheld, IBIS compensates for slight movements, ensuring sharp images, even in low light.

When to Use IBIS:

- **Handheld Photography**: Always turn on IBIS when shooting handheld to reduce blur from shaky hands, especially at slower shutter speeds (e.g., 1/60s or slower).

- **Low Light and Long Exposure**: IBIS is useful for night photography or when you need longer exposure times.

When to Turn Off IBIS:

- **Using a Tripod**: Turn off IBIS when using a tripod to prevent unnecessary movements of the sensor.

- **Lens Stabilization**: If you're using a lens with built-in stabilization, turn off IBIS to avoid conflicts.

Now that you've mastered focus, exposure, and stabilization, it's time to put your knowledge to work. Whether you're shooting portraits, landscapes, or action shots, the Nikon Z5II is ready to help you achieve stunning results.

Taking Better Photos

Ready to take your photography skills to the next level? Whether you're shooting portraits, landscapes, wildlife, or experimenting with creative effects, mastering the basics of composition, camera settings, and technique is key to capturing sharp, professional-looking photos. This guide will walk you through everything, step by step, to help you use your Nikon Z5II like a pro!

Composition Essentials

Composition is the foundation of a great photograph. It's all about how you arrange elements in your frame to create a visually appealing image.

Rule of Thirds

The **Rule of Thirds** is a powerful technique used by photographers to balance their photos. It's simple: Imagine your image divided into nine equal parts using two horizontal and two vertical lines. The idea is to place key elements along these lines or where they intersect.

- **How to Use It**: Turn on the grid lines in your camera settings. These lines will help you position your subject or focal points more naturally.
- **Practical Example**: If you're taking a portrait, align your subject's eyes with the top

horizontal line. This creates a more balanced composition that draws the viewer's attention directly to the subject's face.

Leading Lines

Leading Lines are lines in the image that naturally lead the viewer's eye to the focal point. They could be anything from roads, fences, or rivers to buildings, paths, or railways.

- **How to Use It**: Find natural lines in your environment that lead towards your subject, and position them in a way that guides the viewer's attention.
- **Practical Example**: If you're photographing a road that leads into the distance, position the road so it starts from the bottom corner of your frame and leads the viewer's eye to the horizon.

Symmetry and Patterns

Symmetry and patterns create harmony in a photograph, giving it a sense of balance. These can be found in architecture, nature, and even reflections.

- **How to Use It**: Look for subjects or scenes that are perfectly mirrored, like a building reflected in water or a row of trees.
- **Practical Example**: When photographing a building, position it in the center of your

frame to create symmetry, ensuring both sides of the building are evenly balanced.

Using Creative Picture Controls

The **Creative Picture Controls** on the Nikon Z5II let you apply different looks and styles to your images, adding personal flair without needing extra editing software.

Applying Built-In Presets

Nikon's Creative Picture Controls include presets like Standard, Vivid, and Monochrome that change how your photos look, making them more vibrant, moody, or high-contrast.

- **How to Apply**:
    1. Press the **Menu** button.
    2. Navigate to the **Picture Control** option.
    3. Choose a preset (e.g., Standard, Vivid, Monochrome).
    4. Select **OK** to confirm.
- **Practical Example**: If you're shooting a colorful street scene, try the **Vivid** preset to make the colors pop.

Creating and Saving Custom Styles

If you have a specific style you love, you can create a custom preset. This allows you to save your preferred settings for future use.

- **How to Create**:
    1. Go to the **Menu** and select **Custom Picture Control**.
    2. Adjust settings like sharpness, contrast, brightness, and saturation.
    3. Save the settings as a custom profile.
    4. Next time, simply select your custom style under **Picture Control**.
- **Practical Example**: If you love a soft, dreamy look, lower the sharpness and contrast, then save it as a preset. Whenever you want that look, just select it.

Specialized Shooting Techniques

Each type of photography requires a different approach. Here's how to set up your camera for the best results in various scenarios.

Portrait Setup

When taking portraits, you want your subject to stand out while maintaining a smooth background.

- **Settings**:

- o Use **Wide-Area AF** or **Eye Detection** to ensure sharp focus on your subject's eyes.
- o Select a **wide aperture (f/1.8 - f/5.6)** to blur the background (bokeh effect).
- o Set your **ISO** to a low value (e.g., 100-400) to avoid graininess.
- **Practical Example**: In a portrait, focus on the subject's eyes. The wide aperture will blur the background, ensuring the person is the main focus.

Landscape Setup

For landscapes, you'll want a deep field of focus to keep everything sharp from front to back.

- **Settings**:
  - o Use **Single-Point AF** to focus on a specific point in the scene.
  - o Choose a **small aperture (f/8 - f/16)** for a greater depth of field.
  - o Set **ISO** to 100-200 to reduce noise.
- **Practical Example**: When photographing a mountain range, use a small aperture to keep the entire scene sharp, from the flowers in the foreground to the mountains in the background.

Wildlife and Action Setup

Capturing moving subjects like animals or athletes requires continuous focus tracking.

- **Settings**:
    - o Use **AF-C (Autofocus Continuous)** to keep the subject in focus as it moves.
    - o Choose **Dynamic-Area AF** or **3D Tracking** to track moving subjects.
    - o Use **shutter speeds of 1/500s or faster** to freeze motion.
- **Practical Example**: While photographing a bird in flight, use AF-C and 3D Tracking to follow the bird's movement across the frame.

Low-Light and Night Photography

Low light can be tricky, but the Z5II's ISO sensitivity and image stabilization make it easier to shoot in dark conditions.

- **Settings**:
    - o Use **a low aperture (f/1.4 - f/2.8)** to let in more light.
    - o Set **ISO** to 800-1600 (or higher if necessary) to brighten your image without too much noise.
    - o Use **Image Stabilization (IBIS)** to minimize shake when shooting handheld.
- **Practical Example**: For night photography, increase your ISO slightly and use a wide aperture to let in as much light as possible. Consider using a tripod for long exposures.

Special Features for Sharp, Professional Shots

Pre-Release Capture Mode

This feature allows you to capture photos before you press the shutter button fully. This is especially useful when shooting fast action.

- **How to Use**:
    1. Turn on **Pre-Release Capture** from the menu.
    2. Press the shutter button halfway, and the camera will store images starting from when you first press the button.
    3. When you press the shutter fully, it saves the image along with any frames before that.
- **Practical Example**: If you're photographing a fast-moving athlete, Pre-Release Capture lets you capture the moment just before the action, ensuring you don't miss the perfect shot.

Silent Shutter Mode

This mode helps you take photos without the camera's mechanical shutter sound, which is useful in quiet environments like concerts or wildlife photography.

- **How to Use**:

1. Go to **Silent Shutter** in the camera's settings.
2. Enable the **Silent Shutter Mode**.

- **Practical Example**: In a wildlife setting, use Silent Shutter to take pictures of animals without startling them with the sound of the shutter.

Tips for Sharp, Professional Shots

To get the sharpest, most professional photos, follow these tips:

Autofocus Settings

Make sure to adjust your autofocus settings based on the subject and scene.

- Use **Single-Point AF** for precise focus on a specific area.
- Use **Dynamic-Area AF** for tracking moving subjects.

Best Lenses

The right lens makes a big difference.

- For portraits, use a **50mm f/1.8** lens for beautiful background blur.
- For landscapes, use a **wide-angle lens** like the 16-35mm f/4 for capturing expansive scenes.

Stabilization Techniques

To avoid blur from camera shake:

- **Use a tripod** for stationary shots, especially in low light.
- **Turn on IBIS** (In-Body Image Stabilization) for handheld shots.
- **Use a fast shutter speed** to reduce the effects of camera shake.

With these tips and settings, you're ready to elevate your photography with the Nikon Z5II! Remember, practice makes perfect. Don't hesitate to experiment with different settings and compositions to discover your unique style. Take your time, and enjoy the process.

Video Shooting with the Z5II

The Nikon Z5II is a powerful mirrorless camera, capable of recording high-quality videos. Whether you're vlogging, shooting cinematic footage, or creating content for YouTube, this guide will walk you through everything you need to know to get the best video results.

Video Settings Overview

Choosing Resolution and Frame Rate (4K vs Full HD)

1. **Resolution**: This refers to the clarity of your video. A higher resolution means more detail. You have two main options:
   - **4K (Ultra High Definition)**: Ideal for high-quality, professional video. Perfect for cinematic projects and future-proofing your content.
     - **How to Set 4K**: Go to your camera menu > Video settings > Set the resolution to **4K** (3840x2160).
   - **Full HD (1080p)**: Suitable for most online platforms and everyday use. Easier to work with and less storage-heavy than 4K.

- **How to Set Full HD**: Go to your camera menu > Video settings > Set the resolution to **Full HD (1920x1080)**.

2. **Frame Rate**: This controls how smooth or slow your video looks. Different frame rates give different looks.

   o **24fps (Frames per Second)**: The cinematic frame rate. This is often used for a film-like appearance, especially in movies.
   - **How to Set 24fps**: Go to the video settings > Frame rate > Choose **24fps**.

   o **30fps**: A common frame rate for general video, especially for YouTube and TV. It's slightly smoother than 24fps.
   - **How to Set 30fps**: Go to the video settings > Frame rate > Choose **30fps**.

   o **60fps**: Great for smoother motion, used often in action shots, or if you plan to slow down your video in post-production.
   - **How to Set 60fps**: Go to the video settings > Frame rate > Choose **60fps**.

   o **120fps**: Used for slow-motion video. Capture fast action and slow it down for dramatic effects.
   - **How to Set 120fps**: Go to the video settings > Frame rate >

Choose **120fps** (Full HD resolution is recommended).

Advanced Video Features

10-Bit Internal Recording

1. **What is 10-Bit Recording?**
   - o 10-bit recording offers **more color depth** and **greater dynamic range** compared to 8-bit, allowing for richer colors and smoother transitions in your video.
2. **How to Set 10-Bit Recording**:
   - o In the video settings, make sure your recording format is set to **N-Log** or **ProRes** to enable 10-bit recording.
   - o Go to **Menu > Video settings > 10-bit output > Enable**.

N-RAW and ProRes RAW Setup

1. **What are N-RAW and ProRes RAW?**
   - o These are **high-quality video formats** used by professionals to capture more data in the video file, which gives you greater flexibility in post-production.
   - o **N-RAW** is great for those using **Nikon's N-Log** color profile, while **ProRes RAW** is a popular choice in professional workflows.
2. **How to Set Up N-RAW and ProRes RAW**:

o **ProRes RAW**: Go to **Menu > Video settings > File Format > ProRes RAW**.

o **N-RAW**: Make sure you have an external recorder that supports it (e.g., Atomos Ninja V). Then, connect it to the Z5II and enable the format in the settings.

Focus Peaking and Zebra Patterns

1. **Focus Peaking**:
   o This helps you **see which areas of your video are in focus** by highlighting them in a color (usually red, green, or blue). It's great for manual focus.
   o **How to Enable Focus Peaking**: Go to **Menu > Focus settings > Focus Peaking > Enable**.
2. **Zebra Patterns**:
   o Zebra stripes help you see **overexposed areas** in your shot. These areas will be highlighted with stripes so you can adjust the exposure to avoid losing details in bright spots.
   o **How to Enable Zebra Stripes**: Go to **Menu > Display settings > Zebra Pattern > Enable**.

Audio Recording Essentials

Using External Microphones

1. **Why Use External Microphones?**
   - o The built-in microphone on the Z5II is decent but often picks up unwanted background noise. An external microphone gives you much better audio quality.
2. **How to Connect and Use an External Microphone**:
   - o Plug your external microphone into the **3.5mm microphone input** on the Z5II.
   - o Once connected, go to **Menu > Audio settings > Microphone > Adjust levels**.

Manual Audio Settings

1. **Why Manual Audio Settings?**
   - o You'll want to adjust the audio levels manually to ensure your sound is balanced and clear.
2. **How to Adjust Audio Levels**:
   - o Go to **Menu > Audio settings > Audio level > Adjust using the dial**.
   - o Aim for levels between **-12dB and -6dB** for good audio quality.

Creative Video Techniques

Slow Motion (120fps Full HD)

1. **How Slow Motion Works**:

o By shooting at **120fps**, you can capture slow-motion footage that looks smooth and cinematic.

2. **How to Set Slow Motion**:
   o Go to **Menu > Video settings > Frame rate > 120fps**.
   o Ensure the resolution is set to **Full HD (1920x1080)** to get the best results.

Time-Lapse Movies (Interval Timer Setup)

1. **What is Time-Lapse?**
   o A time-lapse video condenses time by capturing images at specific intervals and playing them back at a faster speed. Great for showing changes over long periods.

2. **How to Set Up a Time-Lapse**:
   o Go to **Menu > Shooting settings > Interval Timer**.
   o Set the interval between shots (e.g., 1 second, 5 seconds) and the total number of frames you want to capture.
   o Press the **Record button** to start capturing your time-lapse.

YouTube and Vlogging Settings

Best Settings for Talking Heads and Action Shots

1. **Talking Heads (Vlogging)**:

- o **Resolution**: Use **Full HD (1080p)** at **30fps** or **24fps**.
- o **Audio**: Ensure you're using an external microphone (like a shotgun mic or lapel mic).
- o **Lighting**: Keep the light source in front of you (natural light or softbox) to avoid shadows on your face.
- o **Focus**: Use **AF-S (Single autofocus)** for sharp focus on your face.

2. **Action Shots**:
   - o **Resolution**: Use **4K** at **60fps** or **120fps** for smooth, slow-motion action.
   - o **Stabilization**: Enable **In-Body Image Stabilization (IBIS)** to reduce camera shake.
   - o **Focus**: Use **AF-C (Continuous autofocus)** to track moving subjects.

Tips for Great Video

1. **Lighting**: Good lighting is key! Always make sure your scene is well-lit to avoid noisy, dark footage.
2. **Stabilization**: Use a tripod or gimbal for steady shots, especially in handheld situations.
3. **Practice**: The best way to get better at video shooting is to practice. Try different settings and techniques to see what works best for your style.

By following these steps, you'll be able to unlock the full potential of your Nikon Z5II for video shooting. Take your time experimenting with different settings to find what works best for your style, and soon, you'll be capturing amazing videos with ease.

Connectivity, Sharing, and Cloud Backup

In today's digital world, it's essential to know how to seamlessly integrate your Nikon Z5II with mobile apps and cloud services for easier control, faster image transfers, and efficient backups. This guide will walk you through everything step-by-step, from setting up remote control to editing your photos and videos on the go. By the end of this guide, you'll be equipped with all the knowledge you need to make the most of your Z5II's connectivity features.

Mobile Integration and App Use

The Nikon Z5II can be connected to several mobile apps, making it easy to control the camera, transfer images, and edit your photos. Two main apps you'll use are **SnapBridge** and **NX Studio**.

Using Nikon Z5II with Mobile Apps (SnapBridge, NX Studio)

SnapBridge and **NX Studio** are the two essential apps you'll be using for mobile integration with your Nikon Z5II.

SnapBridge

SnapBridge is Nikon's dedicated app for wireless image transfer, remote shooting, and camera management.

1. **Download SnapBridge**:
   - Go to the **App Store** for iOS or **Google Play** for Android.
   - Search for **SnapBridge** and install it on your phone or tablet.
2. **Pairing Nikon Z5II with SnapBridge**:

   1. **Turn on the camera** and press the **Menu** button.
   2. Go to **Wi-Fi settings** and enable both **Wi-Fi** and **Bluetooth**.
   3. Open **SnapBridge** on your phone and select **"Connect to Camera"**.
   4. Follow the on-screen instructions to pair the Nikon Z5II with your phone via Bluetooth or Wi-Fi.
   5. Once connected, SnapBridge will show you your camera's live view and allow you to control various camera settings remotely.

3. **Benefits of SnapBridge**:
   - **Image Transfer**: Automatically or manually send photos to your phone.
   - **Remote Shooting**: Use your phone as a remote control to take photos and record videos.

- o **Live View**: View the live camera feed on your phone for precise control.
- o **GPS Tagging**: Use your phone's GPS to tag photos with location data.

NX Studio

NX Studio is Nikon's official software for photo editing and video management, offering more advanced features than SnapBridge.

1. **Download and Install NX Studio**:
   - o Visit **Nikon's website** (www.nikon.com) and download **NX Studio** for **Windows** or **macOS**.
   - o Install the software on your computer following the on-screen instructions.
2. **Transfer Photos from Nikon Z5II to NX Studio**:

   1. Use a **USB cable** to connect your Nikon Z5II to your computer.
   2. Open **NX Studio**.
   3. It will automatically detect the camera, and you'll be able to select the images you want to import.
   4. After importing, you can begin editing your photos in NX Studio.

Remote Control via Mobile Devices (Photography and Video)

Using **SnapBridge**, you can control your Nikon Z5II remotely from your phone, which is perfect for self-portraits, group shots, or when the camera is positioned in hard-to-reach places.

Set Up Remote Control in SnapBridge

1. **Connect the Camera**:
   - Ensure your camera is paired with **SnapBridge** (as explained earlier).
2. **Activate Remote Shooting**:

   1. Open **SnapBridge** on your phone.
   2. Tap on the **Remote Shooting** icon (a camera with a circle).
   3. Choose whether you want to take a **photo** or **video**.
   4. Adjust the camera settings (shutter speed, aperture, ISO) directly from your phone using the app's interface.
   5. Press the **shutter button** on your phone to take a picture or start a video.

Tips for Remote Control

- **Timer Mode**: Set a timer for your shot directly from SnapBridge.

- **Continuous Shooting**: Use the continuous shooting mode if you need multiple shots in a row.
- **Focus**: Adjust the focus remotely before capturing an image.

Easy Image Transfers to Phone or Tablet

Once SnapBridge is set up, transferring photos from your Nikon Z5II to your mobile device is fast and easy.

Enable Image Transfer

1. **Enable Auto Transfer**:
   - In **SnapBridge**, go to **Settings > Auto Transfer** and enable it.
   - This ensures images are automatically transferred to your mobile device when you take them.
2. **Manual Transfer**:

   1. Open **SnapBridge** and tap on the **Gallery** icon to view your photos.
   2. Select the images you want to transfer.
   3. Tap on the **Send to Phone** button to transfer the selected images.
   4. Your photos will appear in your phone's gallery once transferred.

Editing on Mobile

After transferring images to your mobile device, you can use mobile apps to edit your photos and videos.

Best Apps for Mobile Photo Editing

Here are some top apps for editing your Z5II photos:

1. **Adobe Lightroom** (Free and Premium)
    1. Download **Lightroom** from the App Store (iOS) or Google Play (Android).
    2. Import your photos from SnapBridge or your gallery.
    3. Adjust exposure, contrast, color, and sharpness.
    4. Use **Presets** for one-click adjustments.
    5. Export your photos for sharing or saving.
2. **Snapseed** (Free)
    1. Download **Snapseed** from the App Store or Google Play.
    2. Import your image, and use tools like **Tune Image**, **Selective Adjust**, and **Healing**.
    3. Apply **filters** or adjust the photo's **sharpness**.
    4. Save or share your edited photo.

Best Apps for Mobile Video Editing

If you've captured video, these apps are perfect for editing your footage:

1. **Adobe Premiere Rush** (Free and Premium)
   1. Download **Premiere Rush** on your phone.
   2. Import your video footage and trim or cut as needed.
   3. Add transitions, titles, and sound effects.
   4. Export the video directly to social media or save it to your phone.
2. **InShot** (Free and Premium)
   1. Download **InShot** from the App Store or Google Play.
   2. Import your video and use the editing tools to cut, adjust speed, add music, and apply filters.
   3. Export your final video or share it on social media.

Using Nikon Imaging Cloud

Nikon Imaging Cloud is a service that allows you to back up your photos and access them from anywhere. It also offers free editing presets called **Imaging Recipes**.

Set Up Nikon Imaging Cloud

1. **Sign Up**:
   o Go to **Nikon Imaging Cloud** on Nikon's website and sign up for an account.
2. **Linking the Cloud to Your Camera**:
   o After signing up, download the **Nikon Cloud Storage app** on your phone or tablet.
   o Log into your Nikon Imaging Cloud account and link it to your Nikon Z5II.
3. **Upload Photos**:
   o Use **SnapBridge** to upload photos automatically to Nikon Imaging Cloud.
   o You can also upload images manually from your phone's gallery.

Cloud Backup and Free Imaging Recipes

- **Cloud Backup**: The cloud storage ensures your images are safely backed up, so you never lose them.
- **Imaging Recipes**: Nikon offers **Imaging Recipes**—preset settings you can apply to your photos to enhance them quickly.

Firmware Updates and Remote Shooting

Firmware updates keep your camera up-to-date with the latest features and improvements.

How to Update Firmware

1. **Connect to SnapBridge**: Make sure your Nikon Z5II is paired with **SnapBridge**.
2. **Check for Updates**: Open SnapBridge on your phone and go to **Settings** > **Firmware Update**.
3. **Download and Install**: If a firmware update is available, follow the on-screen instructions to download and install it.

Remote Shooting with SnapBridge

1. **Activate Remote Shooting**: Follow the steps earlier to activate **Remote Shooting** in SnapBridge.
2. **Control Settings**: Once activated, you can control the camera's settings, such as **shutter speed, aperture, ISO**, and **focus** from your phone.
3. **Capture Photos/Videos**: Use the phone to remotely trigger the shutter or start/stop video recording.

Now you know how to seamlessly integrate your Nikon Z5II with mobile apps for photo and video editing, cloud backup, and firmware updates. This guide has provided detailed steps to help you connect your camera, transfer images, use mobile editing tools, and back up your content to the cloud.

Post-Processing Your Photos and Videos

In-Depth Photo Post-Processing

Editing RAW Files with Lightroom

When you shoot in RAW, you're getting the most detailed file possible, giving you the flexibility to make significant adjustments without degrading the image quality. Here's how to edit RAW files from the Nikon Z5II using Lightroom:

Import Your Files

1. Open **Lightroom Classic** and click **Import** in the bottom left corner.
2. In the **Import dialog**, navigate to the folder where your RAW files are stored.
3. Select the photos you want to edit, then click **Import**. Your images will appear in the Library module.

Switch to the Develop Module

- At the top of Lightroom, click **Develop** to switch to the editing panel where most adjustments happen.

Adjust the Basic Settings

- **Exposure**: If your photo is too bright or dark, use the **Exposure slider** to adjust the overall brightness. Drag it to the right to brighten, or to the left to darken the image.
- **Contrast**: Increasing contrast adds depth by making dark areas darker and light areas lighter. Adjust the **Contrast slider** to achieve the right balance.
- **White Balance**: Click the **White Balance** dropper tool (the eyedropper icon) and click on a neutral gray area in your image to set the correct white balance automatically. If needed, fine-tune with the **Temp** (temperature) and **Tint** sliders.

Adjust Highlights and Shadows

- **Highlights**: Drag this slider left to bring back details in bright areas (e.g., sky, sunlight).
- **Shadows**: Use this slider to brighten the dark areas of your image without overexposing the highlights.

Fine-Tune Clarity and Texture

- **Clarity**: In the **Presence** section, increase the **Clarity** slider to add more contrast in mid-tones for a sharper look. If you overdo it, it can introduce noise, so use this feature sparingly.
- **Texture**: This slider adjusts the fine details in the image. Use it to emphasize or smooth out

textures like skin, fabric, or landscape features.

Sharpening and Noise Reduction

- Scroll down to the **Detail** panel.
- **Sharpening**: Increase the **Amount** slider to sharpen edges. Adjust **Radius** and **Detail** if needed. Be careful not to over-sharpen as it may create halos around edges.
- **Noise Reduction**: If your image has noise (graininess), use the **Luminance** slider to smooth out the noise. Increase the **Detail** slider to preserve fine details while reducing noise.

Crop and Straighten

- Use the **Crop Overlay** tool (R) to crop your photo and straighten it. Hold the **Shift** key while rotating the image to maintain the aspect ratio.

Lens Corrections

- Scroll down to the **Lens Corrections** panel and check **Enable Profile Corrections**. Lightroom will automatically detect and correct lens distortion, vignetting, and chromatic aberration for your Nikon Z5II lens.

Export Your Image

- Once you're happy with your edits, go to **File** > **Export**.
- Choose a location on your computer, set the file format (JPEG for web, TIFF for high-quality print), and select the **Resolution** (300 DPI for printing, 72 DPI for web).
- Click **Export** to save the edited image.

Editing RAW Files with Capture One

Capture One is another powerful tool for editing RAW files. It offers more advanced features, especially in terms of color grading. Here's how to get started with it:

Import Your Files

1. Open **Capture One** and click on **File** > **Import Images**.
2. Select your RAW files from the Nikon Z5II and click **Import**.

Adjust Basic Settings

- **Exposure**: On the **Exposure** tab, adjust the **Exposure slider** to correct any overexposure or underexposure.
- **White Balance**: Use the **White Balance tool** in the toolbar to correct color temperatures, or manually adjust the **Temperature** and **Tint** sliders.

Color Adjustments

- Capture One allows you to fine-tune the color of individual channels. Go to the **Color** tab and adjust the **Hue**, **Saturation**, and **Lightness (HSL)** for any color range (e.g., make the greens in your landscape photos more vivid).

Sharpening and Noise Reduction

1. **Sharpness**: Use the **Sharpness** slider under the **Detail** tab to enhance the detail in your image.
2. **Noise Reduction**: Under the same tab, use the **Luminance Noise Reduction** to smooth out any graininess.

Layered Edits

- Capture One allows you to create **layers**. For example, if you only want to adjust the sky in your landscape photo, create a new layer, select the **masking tool**, and apply adjustments just to the sky.

Exporting

1. When you're finished, go to **File** > **Export Images**.
2. Choose your desired file format (JPEG, TIFF, PNG), resolution, and destination folder.
3. Click **Export** to save your image.

Video Editing for Z5II Footage

The Z5II shoots amazing 4K video, and with the right editing tools, you can create cinematic videos. Here's a breakdown of editing Z5II footage in **Adobe Premiere Pro** and **DaVinci Resolve**.

Editing Basics in Adobe Premiere Pro

Import Footage

1. Open **Premiere Pro** and create a new project.
2. Click **Import** and select the video files you recorded with your Z5II.

Set Up Your Timeline

1. Drag your footage into the **Timeline**. Premiere will automatically match the sequence settings to your footage's resolution and frame rate.
2. If needed, right-click the sequence, go to **Sequence Settings**, and manually change the resolution or frame rate.

Basic Edits

- **Cutting**: Use the **Razor Tool** (C) to cut clips on the timeline where needed. Click on the timeline where you want the cut to occur.
- **Trimming**: Hover over the edge of the clip and drag to shorten or extend it.

Color Correction

1. Click on the **Color** workspace.
2. Under the **Lumetri Color** panel, adjust:
   - **Basic Correction**: Fix exposure, contrast, white balance.
   - **Creative**: Apply color LUTs for a cinematic look.
   - **Curves**: Adjust brightness and contrast in shadows, midtones, and highlights.

Export Settings

1. Once your video is edited, go to **File > Export > Media**.
2. Choose **H.264** as the format for YouTube videos.
3. Select the **YouTube 1080p Full HD** or **4K** preset depending on the resolution of your video.
4. Click **Export** to render and save your video.

Editing Basics in DaVinci Resolve

Importing Footage

1. Open **DaVinci Resolve** and create a new project.
2. Click **Media** at the bottom, then **Import Media** and select your Z5II footage.

Timeline Setup

1. Drag your clips to the **Timeline**. DaVinci Resolve automatically adjusts to your footage's resolution and frame rate.

Basic Edits

- **Cutting**: Use the **Blade Tool** (B) to slice clips.
- **Trimming**: Hover over the edges of clips in the timeline and drag to trim.

Color Grading

1. Switch to the **Color** workspace.
2. Use the **Lift**, **Gamma**, and **Gain** color wheels to adjust the shadows, midtones, and highlights.
3. **Curves**: Adjust the RGB curves for detailed color adjustments.
4. Use the **LUTs** tab to apply a color look to your video. Experiment with cinematic LUTs.

Exporting

1. After editing, go to the **Deliver** tab.
2. Choose **YouTube 1080p** or **YouTube 4K** depending on your video's resolution.
3. Click **Add to Render Queue**, then click **Start Render** to export your video.

Introduction to Color Grading for Z5II Videos

Basic Color Grading Workflow in Premiere Pro

1. **Correct White Balance**: In the **Lumetri Color** panel, adjust the **White Balance** sliders to remove any color cast from the video.
2. **Adjust Exposure and Contrast**: Use the **Basic Correction** sliders for proper exposure and contrast balance.
3. **Creative Look**: Apply a **LUT (Look-Up Table)** for a specific style or mood (e.g., vintage, cinematic).
4. **Refine Colors**: Use the **Curves** and **Color Wheels** to fine-tune specific areas of your footage for a more cinematic look.

Basic Color Grading in DaVinci Resolve

1. **Lift, Gamma, Gain**: Use the primary color wheels to adjust shadows, midtones, and highlights for a balanced image.
2. **Curves**: Use curves to control brightness and color balance more precisely.
3. **Look-Up Tables (LUTs)**: You can apply predefined LUTs to achieve specific looks quickly. Experiment with different LUTs for various effects (e.g., film looks).

Post-processing your Nikon Z5II photos and videos is where the magic happens! By mastering tools like

Lightroom, Capture One, Premiere Pro, and DaVinci Resolve, you can bring out the true potential of your images and videos.

Real-World Case Studies and Examples

Wedding Photography with the Z5II

Setup and Camera Settings: When you're photographing weddings, your goal is to capture intimate moments, large group shots, and details that tell a beautiful story. The Nikon Z5II is a fantastic tool for wedding photography, thanks to its impressive autofocus, versatile lenses, and excellent low-light performance. Here's how to set it up:

- **Lens Choice**: A prime lens like the **50mm f/1.8** or **85mm f/1.4** is perfect for portraits with beautiful background blur. A wide zoom lens like the **24-70mm f/2.8** is great for group shots and wide-angle scenes.
- **Mode**: Use **Aperture Priority** mode (A on the mode dial) to let the camera automatically adjust shutter speed, giving you the flexibility to adjust the aperture (f-stop) for desired depth of field.
- **ISO**: Keep ISO between **100-800** for daytime and outdoor shots. For low-light indoor venues, you can push it to **1600-3200** without introducing too much noise.
- **Aperture**: Use a wider aperture (f/1.8 or f/2.8) to create a shallow depth of field and beautifully blur the background.

- **Shutter Speed**: Aim for at least **1/200s** for sharp photos, especially when capturing fast movements like walking or dancing.

Challenges:

- **Low Light**: Wedding venues, especially at receptions or in churches, often have low light. The Z5II handles this well, but you may need to bump the ISO or use a faster lens (f/2.8 or lower).
- **Capturing Moments**: Weddings are fast-paced with fleeting moments. The **Eye-Detection AF** (in video and photo) is a great tool to keep the focus on the bride and groom, even when they're moving.

Editing:

- In Lightroom, adjust exposure, contrast, and highlights to ensure the skin tones are natural and vibrant. Use the **graduated filter** to brighten any darker areas without affecting the subject. Apply a light vignette effect for that soft, romantic look.

Street Photography and Storytelling

Setup and Camera Settings: Street photography is about capturing the soul of a city or a spontaneous moment, and the Z5II's compact size and fast autofocus make it an excellent choice. Here's how to set it up:

- **Lens Choice**: A **35mm f/1.8** or **50mm f/1.8** lens is perfect for street photography. These provide a natural field of view and allow you to blend into the scene.
- **Mode**: Use **Shutter Priority** mode (S on the mode dial). Set it to around **1/500s** to freeze motion, especially in busy urban settings.
- **ISO**: Keep ISO low (**100-400**) in daylight. If you're shooting in low light, increase it to **800-1600**, depending on the situation.
- **Aperture**: A middle-range aperture (f/5.6 to f/8) gives you enough depth of field to keep most of your shot in focus while still allowing for some background blur.
- **White Balance**: Keep it on **Auto** unless you're shooting in a controlled light environment.

Challenges:

- **Fast-Moving Subjects**: Street photography often involves fast-moving subjects. The **Z5II's autofocus** is fast enough to keep up, but make sure to use **Continuous AF** to track moving subjects.
- **People's Reactions**: Sometimes, people may notice you photographing them. You may want to avoid drawing attention, so use the camera in **silent shutter mode** to prevent any shutter noise.

Editing:

- After capturing the photos, import them into **Capture One** for more control over color grading and detail enhancement. Use the **Clarity slider** to sharpen the midtones and bring out textures, which is especially useful in street shots.
- Add contrast and adjust the white balance to warm up or cool down the colors depending on the mood you're going for.

Wildlife and Action Photography

Setup and Camera Settings: Capturing wildlife or action shots requires fast shutter speeds, fast autofocus, and the ability to track moving subjects. The Nikon Z5II excels in this with its **Eye-Detection AF** and high frame rate. Here's how to set up:

- **Lens Choice**: A **70-200mm f/2.8** or **300mm f/4** lens is ideal for wildlife. The longer focal lengths allow you to shoot from a distance without disturbing animals.
- **Mode**: Use **Shutter Priority** or **Manual mode** (M) for full control. Set your shutter speed to **1/1000s** or faster to freeze fast movement (such as birds in flight).
- **ISO**: Set ISO based on your available light; it could range from **400** in good daylight to **1600** in low light.
- **Aperture**: Use a wide aperture (f/2.8-f/4) for better subject isolation. This will help blur

the background and make the animal stand out.

- **Focus Mode**: Use **Continuous AF (AF-C)** for tracking moving subjects. Make sure to enable **Wide-Area AF** for better subject coverage.

Challenges:

- **Fast Movement**: Wildlife photography often involves subjects moving quickly, so you need fast autofocus. The Z5II's **Tracking AF** works well, but practice your panning technique to keep moving subjects sharp.
- **Distance**: You'll often need to shoot from a distance, so using a **telephoto lens** and a **tripod** will stabilize your shots.

Editing:

- In **Adobe Lightroom**, increase **shadows** and decrease **highlights** to recover details in bright areas (like sky) and shadowy spots (like under animal fur).
- Apply noise reduction, especially for shots taken at high ISO, and sharpen details to bring out the texture of fur or feathers.

Photo and Video Case Studies: Setup to Final Edit

1. **Wedding Photography**:

- **Setup**: A 50mm f/1.8 lens, Aperture Priority mode, ISO 100, aperture f/2.8.
- **Challenges**: Low-light reception. ISO bumped up to 1600 to avoid noise.
- **Final Edit**: In Lightroom, increased contrast and reduced highlights to preserve skin tones.

2. **Street Photography**:
   - **Setup**: 35mm f/1.8, Shutter Priority mode, ISO 400, aperture f/5.6.
   - **Challenges**: Fast-moving crowds. Continuous AF kept subjects sharp.
   - **Final Edit**: In Capture One, adjusted exposure for midtones and added a slight vignette for focus.

3. **Wildlife Photography**:
   - **Setup**: 70-200mm f/2.8, Shutter Priority mode, ISO 800, aperture f/4.
   - **Challenges**: Shooting at long distances in bright sunlight. Used Continuous AF for tracking.
   - **Final Edit**: In Lightroom, boosted the shadows and clarity to make the animal's features pop.

The Nikon Z5II is a versatile camera that can handle everything from wedding photography to wildlife action shots. Whether you're working in controlled environments like weddings or capturing spontaneous moments in street photography, the Z5II provides the flexibility and performance you need.

By following the detailed steps for each case study, you can approach each type of photography with confidence, knowing how to set up your camera and what adjustments to make during the shoot and in post-processing.

Travel, Care, and Protection for the Nikon Z5II

Traveling with your **Nikon Z5II** is an exciting experience, but protecting your gear from harsh conditions like rain, dust, and extreme temperatures is essential to ensure it lasts. This guide will walk you through the best practices for taking care of your camera during travel, as well as provide tips for cleaning, protecting it from the elements, and maintaining your investment through insurance.

Camera Care During Travel

Best Practices for Travel Photography with the Z5II

Travel photography means you're often on the go and may be exposed to various elements like humidity, dirt, or even harsh sunlight. Taking a few steps to protect your Nikon Z5II will help it perform optimally and last longer.

1. **Use a Camera Bag with Proper Padding**:
    - **Why**: Your camera is precious and can easily get scratched or damaged while traveling. A padded camera bag will cushion it from bumps, drops, and any accidental impacts.

- o **Recommendation**: Look for a bag with dividers, water-resistant material, and enough space for extra lenses, batteries, and memory cards.

2. **Remove the Lens When Not in Use**:
   - o **Why**: Leaving the lens attached for long periods can expose the lens mount to dust and dirt, potentially causing damage.
   - o **Tip**: If you're not using your Z5II, take off the lens and store it separately in a lens pouch or the bag's padded compartment.

3. **Protect the LCD Screen**:
   - o **Why**: The screen can get scratched or damaged easily when it's constantly exposed to your bag or other gear.
   - o **Solution**: Use a **screen protector** to prevent scratches and smudges. This will keep the display in top condition for your shots.

Protecting Your Z5II in Extreme Conditions (Rain, Cold, Dust)

The Z5II is designed with weather sealing to protect it from some elements, but it still requires additional care in harsh conditions.

1. **In the Rain:**
   - o **Weather Protection Gear**: Even though the Z5II is weather-sealed, it's a good idea to use a **rain cover** or a

weatherproof camera sleeve for additional protection.

- o **Use a Lens Hood**: A **lens hood** not only reduces lens flare but also adds an extra layer of protection from rain droplets hitting the lens.
- o **Tip**: Always keep a **microfiber cloth** in your bag to wipe away water from the lens and camera body.

2. **In the Cold (Sub-Zero Temperatures):**
   - o **Avoid Rapid Temperature Changes**: Moving from a warm area (like inside a restaurant) to the cold can cause condensation to form inside your camera. To prevent this, place your camera inside a plastic bag before going from a warm environment to a cold one. This helps prevent the internal temperature change.
   - o **Battery Life**: Cold weather drains batteries quickly. Always carry extra batteries and keep them in a pocket close to your body to keep them warm. **Lithium-ion batteries** perform poorly in extreme cold, so having backups is key.
   - o **Don't Touch the Lens with Bare Hands**: Cold weather can cause moisture or frost to form. Always handle your camera with gloves, especially when taking it in and out of bags.

3. **In Dusty or Sandy Environments:**
    - **Lens Protection**: Use a **UV filter** or clear protective filter on the front of your lens to protect it from dust, sand, and scratches.
    - **Avoid Changing Lenses Outdoors**: Changing lenses in a dusty or windy environment can cause particles to get inside the camera body, potentially damaging the sensor. If you must change lenses, do it inside your camera bag or a sheltered space.

Cleaning Your Z5II Properly

Keeping your Nikon Z5II clean is essential to maintaining its performance, especially if you're traveling in challenging conditions. Here's how to properly clean your camera:

Sensor Care:

1. **When to Clean the Sensor**: If you notice spots or dust marks in your images (especially in high aperture shots with clear skies or backgrounds), it's time to clean the sensor.
2. **How to Clean the Sensor**:
    - Turn your camera off, remove the lens, and set the camera to **sensor cleaning mode**. This will lock the mirror up (for DSLRs, but the Z5II is

mirrorless, so it's different) and allow the sensor to be cleaned.

- o Use a **blower bulb** to gently blow off loose dust. Make sure not to touch the sensor with the blower or your fingers.
- o If you need more thorough cleaning, use a **sensor cleaning swab** with a sensor-safe cleaning solution. Be gentle, and always use light pressure to avoid damaging the sensor.

Exterior Care:

1. **Lens Cleaning**:
   - o Always use a **lens brush** or a **microfiber cloth** to clean the front and rear elements of your lens. Avoid using tissues or rough cloths that could scratch the glass.
   - o For stubborn smudges, use a lens cleaning solution and a microfiber cloth to clean the lens in a circular motion.
2. **Camera Body Cleaning**:
   - o Use a **soft, dry microfiber cloth** to wipe down the body of your camera. This will remove dust and fingerprints. Avoid using harsh chemicals that could damage the camera's finish.
   - o **Blow away dust** from ports, buttons, and the viewfinder with a **blower**

bulb to prevent dust from getting inside the camera body.

Insurance and Warranty Advice

Your camera is a big investment, so protecting it with insurance is a wise choice. Here's how you can safeguard your Z5II:

Camera Insurance:

1. **Why You Need It**: Cameras are susceptible to accidents, theft, or damage, especially when traveling. Insurance ensures that you can replace or repair your Z5II in case of an unfortunate event.
2. **What to Look for in Insurance**: Choose a policy that covers:
   o **Accidental damage** (drops, spills, etc.)
   o **Theft or loss** during travel
   o **Natural disasters** (like floods or earthquakes)
   o **Repair costs** for physical damage or sensor issues.

Many photography gear-specific insurance providers exist, such as **PPA Insurance** or **PhotoCare**, but general providers also offer coverage for electronics.

3. **Warranty Advice**:
   o Nikon offers a **2-year warranty** for the Z5II. Always keep your purchase

receipt in case you need to make a warranty claim.

- o Make sure to register your Nikon Z5II on the official Nikon website to activate your warranty.

Travel Photography Tips Specific to the Z5II

Taking your Z5II on a trip is exciting, and it's an excellent choice for travel photography. Here are some tips to help you get the best shots:

1. **Capture Candid Moments**: Use the **silent shutter mode** to capture candid moments without disturbing people. This is especially useful for street photography or when you want to take photos discreetly.
2. **Use the LCD Screen and EVF**: The Z5II's **Electronic Viewfinder (EVF)** and **tilting LCD screen** are great for composing shots in tight or tricky angles, like while shooting over a crowd or while lying on the ground for a low-angle shot.
3. **Wide-Angle Lenses**: For breathtaking landscapes, pack a **16-35mm f/4 lens** or a similar wide-angle lens. This will give you the flexibility to capture stunning vistas and architectural shots with the Z5II's impressive dynamic range.
4. **Shooting in RAW**: Always shoot in **RAW** format when traveling to ensure maximum

flexibility in post-processing. RAW files retain more image information, which is especially useful when you need to adjust exposure or recover shadows and highlights.

5. **Backup Your Photos Regularly**: During long travels, always back up your photos. Consider using a **portable hard drive** or **cloud storage** for extra safety. You can also use the **Nikon SnapBridge** app to wirelessly back up your images to your mobile device.

Taking care of your Nikon Z5II during travel and harsh conditions is all about being prepared and proactive. By following these detailed steps for protecting your camera, cleaning it properly, and ensuring it's covered by insurance, you can confidently enjoy your travels without worrying about potential damage. Combine that with some smart photography tips, and you'll be well on your way to capturing stunning travel photos and videos for years to come.

Advanced Techniques for the Nikon Z5II

Customizing Buttons and Menus

The Nikon Z5II allows you to assign custom functions to buttons, enabling a smoother, personalized shooting experience. This is especially useful when you want to quickly access frequently used settings, without digging through the menu.

Step-by-Step:

1. **Access the Custom Button Settings:**
   - Press the **Menu** button on the back of your camera.
   - Navigate to the **Custom Settings Menu** (the pencil icon).
   - Scroll down and select **Controls**.
   - In the "Custom Controls" menu, select the button you want to customize (e.g., Fn button, AE-L button, etc.).
2. **Assign a Function:**
   - Once you've selected the button, you'll see a list of available functions you can assign.
   - Scroll through the list and choose a function that will improve your workflow, such as **ISO**, **White Balance**, or **Focus Area**.
   - Press **OK** to save your selection.

Tips for Custom Buttons:

- **Fn Button Customization:** For example, you might want to set **ISO** to the Fn button for quick adjustments during low-light scenarios.
- **AE-L/AF-L Button:** Consider assigning the **AF-ON** function here for back-button focusing, which improves focus control.

Saving Custom Shooting Modes (U1, U2, U3)

The Z5II allows you to store custom shooting settings for different situations. Using the **U1**, **U2**, and **U3** modes, you can quickly switch between various preset configurations without having to manually adjust settings every time.

Step-by-Step:

1. **Set the Desired Parameters:**
   o Choose the settings you want to save (e.g., aperture, shutter speed, ISO, white balance, focus mode, etc.).
2. **Save the Settings:**
   o Once you've adjusted everything, press the **Mode** dial on the top of the camera to switch to either **U1**, **U2**, or **U3**.
   o Go to **Menu → Custom Settings → Save Settings to U1/U2/U3**.

- Select the preset (U1, U2, or U3) to store the settings.
3. **Switch Between Modes:**
   - Turn the **Mode dial** to quickly switch between your saved configurations, ideal for switching between portrait, landscape, or night photography setups.

Focus Stacking (Focus Shift Shooting)

Focus stacking allows you to capture images with a large depth of field, which is great for macro photography or landscape shots with incredible detail from foreground to background.

Step-by-Step:

1. **Activate Focus Shift Mode:**
   - Press the **Menu** button, go to **Custom Settings** → **Shoot (Photo)** → **Focus Shift Shooting**.
   - Enable **Focus Shift** and adjust settings for the number of shots (more shots = better depth of field).
2. **Set Your Focus Range:**
   - Set the **Start/End Focus Points**. The camera will automatically move the focus from near to far, capturing a series of images.
3. **Shoot Your Series:**

- After selecting all the options, press the shutter to begin the shooting sequence. The camera will capture multiple shots at different focus points.

4. **Post-Processing:**
   - Import the images into editing software like **Adobe Photoshop** and use the **Stacking** feature to combine all the focus points into one sharp image.

Dual SD Card Strategies

The Z5II has dual SD card slots, giving you flexibility for storing your images and videos. You can set up the cards for backup or for different file types (e.g., RAW + JPEG).

Step-by-Step:

1. **Backup Mode:**
   - Press the **Menu** button → **Setup Menu** → **Slot Settings** → **Backup**.
   - This ensures that every image you take is saved to both SD cards. It's a good safety net in case one card fails.

2. **Overflow Mode:**
   - In **Overflow Mode**, once the first card fills up, the second card automatically starts saving new images.

- o Choose **Overflow** from the Slot Settings if you're shooting a lot of photos (e.g., at a wedding or event).
3. **RAW+JPEG Mode:**
    - o If you prefer to have both a high-quality RAW file and a smaller JPEG, set **RAW + JPEG** on one card, while saving only the RAW files on the other.
    - o Go to **Setup Menu** → **Slot Settings** → **RAW/JPEG** and assign them to different slots.

Pixel Shift Shooting (Future Firmware-Ready)

The Z5II supports **Pixel Shift** shooting, which takes multiple images with slight shifts of the sensor to capture extra detail and reduce noise. This feature is not yet enabled but will be available in a future firmware update.

Step-by-Step (when available):

1. **Enable Pixel Shift Mode:**
    - o Once the feature is available via firmware update, access the **Custom Menu** and enable **Pixel Shift** mode.
2. **Capture Multiple Images:**
    - o The camera will capture a series of images, shifting the sensor incrementally with each shot.

3. **Combine in Post-Processing:**
   - Use software such as **Nikon's NX Studio** or other compatible software to combine the images and create an ultra-detailed, noise-reduced photograph.

Astrophotography with the Z5II

The Z5II offers great potential for astrophotography, with its high-resolution sensor and customizable settings. Capturing the stars, Milky Way, and other celestial objects requires a good understanding of settings.

Step-by-Step:

1. **Use Manual Mode:**
   - Set your camera to **Manual Mode (M)** for full control over exposure.
2. **Adjust Your Settings:**
   - **Shutter Speed:** Set it to around **15-25 seconds** (longer might result in star trails).
   - **Aperture:** Use a **wide aperture** (f/2.8 or wider).
   - **ISO:** Start with **ISO 1600-3200**, and adjust based on results.
3. **Use a Wide-Angle Lens:**
   - Choose a **wide-angle lens** (e.g., 14mm-24mm), as it allows you to capture more of the sky.
4. **Set Focus to Infinity:**

- o Switch the lens focus to **infinity**. If your lens doesn't have an infinity focus marker, manually focus on a distant light before shooting.

5. **Shoot in RAW:**
   - o Shooting in **RAW** gives you more flexibility during post-processing to adjust exposure, contrast, and noise reduction.

6. **Use a Tripod and Remote Shutter:**
   - o A sturdy tripod is essential to prevent camera shake. Consider using the **remote shutter release** or the **camera's self-timer** for minimal vibration.

By following these steps, you'll be able to unlock the full potential of your Nikon Z5II, whether you're shooting portraits, landscapes, action, or astrophotography. The customizable settings, focus stacking, dual card strategies, and specialized modes make the Z5II a versatile tool for both beginners and advanced photographers.

Recommended Accessories

The Nikon Z5II is a powerful and versatile mirrorless camera that excels in a wide variety of photography and video applications. To truly get the best out of it, you'll need the right accessories to complement its features. This buyer's guide will help you choose the best lenses, SD cards, tripods, microphones, lights, lens adapters, and bags tailored to the needs of both beginners and advanced users.

Best Lenses for Nikon Z5II

The Nikon Z5II supports the new **Z-mount**, which offers excellent image quality, fast autofocus, and broad aperture ranges. Here are some of the best lenses you can pair with your Z5II, from versatile options to specialized choices.

For Beginners:

Nikon Nikkor Z 24-70mm f/4 S

- **Why It's Great:** A versatile zoom lens that covers a wide range of focal lengths from 24mm (wide-angle) to 70mm (short telephoto), ideal for everything from landscapes to portraits.
- **Key Features:**
  - Compact and lightweight
  - Excellent image quality

- o Smooth autofocus for both stills and video
- **What to Look For:** A lens like this is perfect for new photographers as it gives you a "one-lens solution" for most situations.

Nikon Nikkor Z 50mm f/1.8 S

- **Why It's Great:** A prime lens that excels in low light and provides a beautiful bokeh for portraits. It's an affordable option with fantastic image quality.
- **Key Features:**
  - o Fast f/1.8 aperture
  - o Sharp at all apertures
  - o Great for portraits and low-light photography
- **What to Look For:** This is a must-have for portrait photographers and anyone looking to experiment with shallow depth of field.

For Advanced Users:

Nikon Nikkor Z 24-70mm f/2.8 S

- **Why It's Great:** A pro-grade version of the 24-70mm f/4. This lens has a wider aperture, making it great for low-light situations and producing more background blur.
- **Key Features:**
  - o Wide f/2.8 aperture for better subject isolation
  - o Superb image quality and sharpness

- o Dust and moisture-resistant
- **What to Look For:** If you need a faster zoom lens with more control over depth of field, this is an excellent upgrade.

Nikon Nikkor Z 70-200mm f/2.8 VR S

- **Why It's Great:** Perfect for wildlife, sports, or event photography, this telephoto lens lets you zoom in on distant subjects while maintaining sharpness.
- **Key Features:**
  - o Fast f/2.8 aperture for low light and creamy background blur
  - o Vibration Reduction (VR) for steady handheld shots
  - o Excellent autofocus
- **What to Look For:** If you plan on shooting action, wildlife, or need a zoom lens for professional events, this lens is a great choice.

Best SD Cards, Batteries, and Chargers

Having reliable SD cards, spare batteries, and a good charger is essential for long shooting sessions or travel.

SD Cards:

SanDisk Extreme Pro SD UHS-II 64GB

- **Why It's Great:** Fast read and write speeds ensure quick data transfer, and it's UHS-II rated for 4K video recording.
- **Key Features:**
  - High-speed performance (300MB/s read and 260MB/s write)
  - Reliable for 4K video and high-resolution stills
- **What to Look For:** Make sure to choose an SD card with UHS-II compatibility for maximum performance with the Z5II.

Lexar Professional 1000x SDXC UHS-II 64GB

- **Why It's Great:** Another solid choice for video shooters, offering reliable performance for continuous burst shooting or video.
- **Key Features:**
  - 150MB/s write speed for fast burst shooting
  - Ideal for both photography and video recording
- **What to Look For:** This card is a great alternative if you need an affordable UHS-II card with excellent performance.

Batteries:

Nikon EN-EL15c Rechargeable Li-ion Battery

- **Why It's Great:** The Z5II uses the EN-EL15c battery, which offers decent power for extended shoots.

- **Key Features:**
    - Long-lasting power
    - Works well with Nikon's fast-charging system
- **What to Look For:** Always have at least one spare battery for longer shoots or travel, as mirrorless cameras tend to consume more battery than DSLRs.

Chargers:

Nikon MH-25a Quick Charger

- **Why It's Great:** A high-quality, fast charger that works directly with the EN-EL15c battery.
- **Key Features:**
    - Charges battery efficiently
    - Compact design for easy portability
- **What to Look For:** Ensure compatibility with the EN-EL15c battery to keep your gear charged while on the go.

Recommended Tripods, Gimbals, and Stabilizers

A good tripod or gimbal is essential for capturing stable shots, whether you're shooting landscapes, portraits, or videos.

Tripods:

Manfrotto MT190XPRO3 Aluminum Tripod

- **Why It's Great:** A solid tripod with a versatile design that offers great stability for both photography and video.
- **Key Features:**
  - Adjustable center column for low-angle shots
  - Sturdy construction
  - Easy-to-use leg locks
- **What to Look For:** Make sure the tripod you choose supports the weight of your Z5II and your lens combination.

Peak Design Travel Tripod

- **Why It's Great:** A lightweight, compact tripod that's perfect for travel without sacrificing stability.
- **Key Features:**
  - Carbon fiber for reduced weight
  - Foldable and compact for easy storage
- **What to Look For:** If portability is important to you, this is a top choice for travel photographers.

Gimbals/Stabilizers:

DJI Ronin-SC Gimbal Stabilizer

- **Why It's Great:** Perfect for video creators who need smooth, cinematic footage.
- **Key Features:**
  - Lightweight yet powerful
  - Easy setup and intuitive controls
- **What to Look For:** If you're shooting video, this gimbal will make sure your footage stays steady, even when moving around.

External Microphones for Video Creators

The built-in microphone on the Z5II may not offer the best audio quality for professional video, so using an external mic is essential.

Rode VideoMic Pro+

- **Why It's Great:** Excellent sound quality and ease of use make it the top choice for filmmakers.
- **Key Features:**
  - Directional microphone to capture clear sound
  - Built-in shock mount to reduce handling noise
  - Automatic power on/off feature
- **What to Look For:** Great for vloggers and content creators who want clear audio for video.

Shure VP83F LensHopper

- **Why It's Great:** Offers high-quality audio and is designed for cameras with a shoe mount.
- **Key Features:**
  - Compact size
  - High-pass filter to eliminate low-frequency noise
- **What to Look For:** Ideal for content creators who need a portable, high-quality microphone.

Useful LED Lights, Lens Adapters, and Camera Bags

Lighting and lens adapters can make a huge difference in your shots, while a good camera bag ensures that all your gear stays protected.

LED Lights:

Neewer 660 LED Video Light

- **Why It's Great:** A versatile light that can be used for both photography and video, providing soft, adjustable lighting.
- **Key Features:**
  - Adjustable brightness and color temperature
  - Compact and lightweight
- **What to Look For:** Ideal for video creators looking to enhance their lighting setup.

Lens Adapters:

Fotodiox Pro Lens Mount Adapter (Nikon F to Z-mount)

- **Why It's Great:** If you have older Nikon F-mount lenses, this adapter allows you to use them with your Z5II.
- **Key Features:**
    - Solid build quality
    - Allows the use of Nikon DSLR lenses on the Z5II
- **What to Look For:** Essential if you already own F-mount lenses and want to use them with the Z5II without losing image quality.

Camera Bags:

Peak Design Everyday Backpack 20L

- **Why It's Great:** A spacious and customizable bag that offers excellent protection for your Z5II and accessories.
- **Key Features:**
    - Dividers to organize gear
    - Weatherproof material
- **What to Look For:** Ideal for photographers who need a well-organized, durable bag for travel and daily use.

Lowepro ProTactic 350 AW

- **Why It's Great:** A robust bag that can carry all your equipment while keeping it safe from the elements.
- **Key Features:**
  - Adjustable dividers for customizable compartments
  - Weather-resistant cover
- **What to Look For:** If you're traveling or shooting in tough conditions, this bag will keep your gear protected.

Choosing the right accessories for your Nikon Z5II can make a world of difference in the quality of your work. Whether you're just getting started or already have experience, these recommended lenses, SD cards, tripods, microphones, lights, adapters, and bags will help you get the most out of your camera. Invest in the right accessories to elevate your photography and videography to the next level!

MASTER YOUR CRAFT

Whether you're a beginner or an experienced photographer looking to push your skills further, continuous learning and practice are key. This guide will help you master your craft with practical challenges, assignments, editing tips, and ways to connect with the broader photography community. Let's dive in!

30-Day Photography Challenge for Skill Building

One of the best ways to rapidly improve your photography is through focused practice. A 30-day challenge helps you build specific skills by committing to daily assignments that push your creativity and technique. Here's a breakdown of what you can focus on each week:

Week 1: Basic Composition & Lighting

- **Day 1-3:** Experiment with the **Rule of Thirds**. Shoot a variety of subjects, from landscapes to portraits, keeping the subject placed along the gridlines.
- **Day 4-6:** Work on **framing** your shots. Use objects like doorways, windows, or trees to create a natural frame around your subject.
- **Day 7:** Explore **natural light**. Pay attention to how different times of the day (morning,

midday, evening) affect the mood and quality of light.

Week 2: Exposure & Focus Techniques

- **Day 8-10:** Learn the basics of **exposure** by adjusting your shutter speed, aperture, and ISO. Try shooting in manual mode to control each setting.
- **Day 11-13:** Experiment with **depth of field**. Shoot wide open at f/1.8 to get a blurry background, and then stop down to f/11 to see how everything in the frame stays sharp.
- **Day 14:** Try **focus techniques** like **selective focus** (focus on a single subject and blur the background) or **focus stacking** for increased sharpness in macro shots.

Week 3: Creative Styles & Subject Focus

- **Day 15-17:** Focus on **portraiture**. Play with posing, lighting, and expressions to make your portraits more engaging.
- **Day 18-20:** Dive into **landscape photography**. Focus on wide-angle shots, leading lines, and using the foreground to add depth.
- **Day 21:** Try **street photography**. Capture candid moments in public spaces, paying attention to interesting compositions, contrasts, and storytelling.

Week 4: Post-Processing & Workflow

- **Day 22-24:** Learn basic post-processing with **Lightroom**. Start by correcting exposure, adjusting contrast, and fine-tuning color balance.
- **Day 25-27:** Experiment with more advanced techniques in **Photoshop**. Try using layers, adjustment brushes, and blending modes to enhance your photos.
- **Day 28-30:** Create a final portfolio of your best shots from the challenge. Reflect on what you've learned and how your photography has improved.

Weekly Creative Photography Assignments

While the 30-day challenge helps you build foundational skills, ongoing creative assignments will keep you sharp and inspired. Here are some weekly assignments you can use to expand your creativity:

- **Black and White Photography:** Challenge yourself to see the world in monochrome. Pay attention to shadows, textures, and contrasts that might not be as noticeable in color.
- **Motion Blur:** Experiment with long exposures or slow shutter speeds to capture motion in your photos. Try shooting moving water, people walking, or vehicles in motion.

- **Reflections:** Find reflective surfaces such as puddles, glass, or mirrors, and use them creatively to add depth and symmetry to your shots.
- **Color Exploration:** Pick a color (or a combination of colors) and use it as the dominant theme in your photos. It could be a single color or complementary colors that create harmony in your images.
- **Night Photography:** Challenge yourself to capture the beauty of the night. Experiment with light trails, cityscapes, and even the stars using long exposures.

Introduction to Advanced Editing (Lightroom and Photoshop Basics)

Post-processing is an essential part of modern photography, allowing you to enhance your images and correct imperfections. Here's a beginner-friendly introduction to editing in **Lightroom** and **Photoshop**:

Lightroom Basics:

- **Importing & Organizing:** Start by importing your photos into Lightroom. Organize your images using Collections or Folders to keep everything neat.
- **Basic Adjustments:**

- Exposure: Adjust the exposure slider to correct the overall brightness of your image.
- Contrast & Clarity: Enhance midtones and texture with the contrast slider, and use clarity to add sharpness to details.
- White Balance: Adjust the temperature and tint to make your image feel warmer or cooler, depending on the mood you want to create.

- **Cropping & Straightening:** Use the Crop tool to improve composition and straighten horizons or vertical lines.
- **Color Grading:** Use the HSL (Hue, Saturation, Luminance) panel to selectively adjust colors for a more dynamic or moody look.

Photoshop Basics:

- **Layers & Masks:** Photoshop operates with layers, allowing you to apply effects, adjustments, and edits non-destructively. Use masks to apply changes to specific areas of the image.
- **Healing Brush & Clone Stamp:** These tools are perfect for removing unwanted elements in your photos, like blemishes or distractions.
- **Dodge and Burn:** Use these tools to brighten highlights or darken shadows, giving your photos more depth and dimension.

- **Advanced Techniques:** Once you're comfortable with the basics, explore advanced techniques like compositing, frequency separation (for retouching), and sharpening.

Joining the Nikon Z Community and Online Resources

Being part of a photography community can help you grow, get feedback, and stay inspired. Here are some ways to connect with other Nikon Z users and get the most out of your Nikon Z5II:

Nikon Z Community:

- **Online Forums & Groups:** Join Nikon's official forums, as well as Facebook or Reddit groups dedicated to Nikon Z series cameras. These communities are a great place to share your work, ask questions, and learn from others.
- **Workshops and Meetups:** Look for online or in-person workshops, where you can learn from professionals and meet fellow photographers. Nikon often hosts events and seminars focused on their Z series cameras.
- **Social Media:** Follow Nikon's official social media pages and use hashtags like #NikonZ to see what other photographers are creating. It's a great way to get inspired and stay up-

to-date on new product releases and techniques.

Online Resources:

- **YouTube Tutorials:** There are countless YouTube channels offering tutorials for Nikon cameras and photography in general. Channels like **Nikon's official channel**, **Mango Street**, and **Peter McKinnon** provide excellent content to improve your shooting and editing skills.
- **Photography Blogs & Websites:** Websites like **Fstoppers**, **PetaPixel**, and **Digital Photography School** offer valuable articles and tips for photographers of all skill levels.
- **Nikon's User Manual & Support:** Make sure to regularly check Nikon's official website for detailed user manuals, firmware updates, and tips specific to the Z5II. It's a great resource for troubleshooting and learning about new features.

Mastering your craft as a photographer is a lifelong journey that involves continuous learning, practice, and community engagement. Whether you're diving into a 30-day challenge, taking on weekly assignments, or learning advanced editing techniques, every step you take will bring you closer to your creative goals. Don't forget to join online communities and stay updated with the latest resources to continue improving. With patience and dedication, you'll soon see a noticeable difference in the quality of your work. Keep shooting, keep editing, and most importantly—keep learning!

Bonus

Quick Reference Cheat Sheets for Nikon Z5II

30 Most Useful Shortcuts and Tips

Here are 30 essential shortcuts and tips for mastering your Nikon Z5II quickly and effectively:

Shortcut/Tip	Function
Fn Button (Customizable)	Assign frequently used functions (e.g., white balance, ISO, etc.).
U1/U2/U3 Custom Modes	Save your preferred settings for quick access.
ISO Button	Adjust ISO without entering the menu.
Aperture Priority Mode (A)	Control aperture while letting the camera automatically adjust shutter.
Shutter Priority Mode (S)	Control shutter speed while camera adjusts aperture.
Manual Mode (M)	Fully control both shutter speed and aperture.
Auto Focus (AF) Mode	Switch between Single Point, Dynamic Area, and Wide Area AF.

Shortcut/Tip	Function
Back Button Focus (BBF)	Assign focus to a button (often the AF-ON button) for more precise control.
RAW+JPEG	Capture both RAW and JPEG simultaneously for flexibility.
Touchscreen Focus	Use the touchscreen to select focus points or trigger the shutter.
Exposure Compensation	Adjust exposure by turning the exposure compensation dial.
White Balance (WB)	Set custom white balance or use presets for different lighting.
Continuous Shooting Mode	Press the shutter for continuous high-speed bursts.
Live View (LV)	Use for composing images via the LCD screen.
Viewfinder (EVF)	Switch to the electronic viewfinder for more precise control.
Menu Button (Red Circle)	Quick access to the main camera menu.
Play Button	Review your photos and videos instantly.
ISO Auto Sensitivity Control	Set ISO to auto and adjust the max sensitivity for noise control.

Shortcut/Tip	Function
AEL/AFL Button	Lock exposure and/or focus independently.
Self-Timer	Set a self-timer for group photos or self-portraits.
Zoom in (Magnify Button)	Quickly zoom into your image for finer detail review.
HDR Mode	Enable for higher dynamic range shots.
Highlight Weighted Metering	Prioritize highlights for more balanced exposure in challenging light.
Tilt Screen	Adjust the screen for higher or lower angle shooting.
Zebra Pattern	Display highlight warnings in overexposed areas.
Focus Peaking	Highlight in-focus areas with a colored outline in manual focus mode.
File Format	Choose between RAW, JPEG, or TIFF for image quality.
Nikon SnapBridge App	Connect to your phone for quick photo transfer and remote control.
Touch AF	Tap the screen to instantly focus on your subject.
Interval Timer	Shoot time-lapse photography by setting a timed interval.

Shortcut/Tip	Function
Depth of Field Preview Button	Preview depth of field in real-time before taking the shot.

Pro Settings Recipes for Different Scenarios

Here are optimized settings for a variety of common photography scenarios:

Portrait Photography:

- **Mode:** Aperture Priority (A)
- **Aperture:** f/1.8 - f/2.8 (for shallow depth of field)
- **ISO:** 100-400 (adjust based on lighting conditions)
- **Shutter Speed:** 1/125s or faster (to prevent motion blur)
- **White Balance:** Custom or Daylight
- **Focus Mode:** Single-Point AF (focused on the subject's eyes)

Landscape Photography:

- **Mode:** Aperture Priority (A)
- **Aperture:** f/8 - f/16 (for sharpness across the frame)
- **ISO:** 100 (keep it low for maximum detail)
- **Shutter Speed:** Use a tripod and adjust for desired exposure

- **White Balance:** Daylight or Custom (to match the scene)
- **Focus Mode:** Manual Focus (for precise control)

Sports Photography:

- **Mode:** Shutter Priority (S)
- **Shutter Speed:** 1/1000s or faster (for freezing motion)
- **ISO:** Auto or 800-1600 (to maintain proper exposure)
- **Aperture:** Wide (f/2.8 - f/4) for shallow depth of field
- **Focus Mode:** Continuous AF (Tracking mode)
- **Burst Mode:** High-speed continuous shooting

Video (Vlogging or Content Creation):

- **Mode:** Manual (M)
- **Shutter Speed:** 1/50s (for cinematic video look)
- **Aperture:** f/2.8 - f/4 (for shallow depth of field)
- **ISO:** 800-1600 (depending on available light)
- **White Balance:** Custom or set to match light source
- **Focus Mode:** Continuous AF with Face Detection

Quick Setup Guides for Portraits, Landscapes, Sports, and Video

Portrait Photography Setup:

1. Set the **camera to Aperture Priority** mode (A).
2. Select a **wide aperture (f/1.8 to f/2.8)** for a shallow depth of field.
3. Adjust the **ISO** to 100-400, depending on ambient light.
4. **Single-point AF** to focus on the subject's eyes.
5. Use **natural light** or a softbox for studio portraits.
6. **Shoot at a higher shutter speed (1/125s or faster)** to avoid camera shake.

Landscape Photography Setup:

1. Switch to **Aperture Priority mode** (A).
2. Set **aperture to f/8 or f/11** for sharp focus from front to back.
3. Use **ISO 100** to prevent noise.
4. Set the **white balance** to Daylight for accurate colors.
5. Mount the camera on a **tripod** for stability.
6. Use **manual focus** or live view to get precise focus on the landscape.

Sports Photography Setup:

1. Set the **camera to Shutter Priority (S)** mode.
2. Set **shutter speed to 1/1000s or faster** to freeze motion.
3. Choose **continuous autofocus** to track moving subjects.
4. Use **ISO Auto** or set the ISO to 800-1600 depending on the lighting.
5. Enable **high-speed continuous shooting** for capturing fast actions.

Video Setup:

1. Set the camera to **Manual mode (M)** for full control.
2. Choose a **shutter speed of 1/50s** for smooth video.
3. Set the **aperture to f/2.8 to f/4** for a shallow depth of field.
4. Use **ISO 800-1600** for well-exposed footage.
5. Ensure **Continuous AF** is enabled with **Face Detection**.
6. **Use a tripod or gimbal** for stable video recording.

These cheat sheets provide quick, easy-to-access information for Nikon Z5II users. Whether you're a beginner or a pro, this guide should help you navigate your gear, make quick adjustments, and improve your workflow.

Appendix

Glossary of Photography Terms

Here are some essential photography terms that will help you understand and navigate your Nikon Z5II better:

- **Aperture (f-stop):** The opening in the lens that controls how much light enters the camera. The smaller the number (f/1.8), the larger the opening and the more light that enters. It also affects the depth of field, or how much of the scene is in focus.
- **Shutter Speed:** The amount of time the camera's sensor is exposed to light. It is measured in seconds or fractions of a second. Faster shutter speeds (e.g., 1/1000s) freeze motion, while slower speeds (e.g., 1/30s) can introduce motion blur.
- **ISO:** The sensitivity of your camera's sensor to light. A lower ISO (e.g., 100) is ideal for bright conditions, while higher ISOs (e.g., 1600, 3200) are used in low-light situations but may introduce noise or grain.
- **Exposure Triangle:** The relationship between aperture, shutter speed, and ISO that affects the exposure of an image. Balancing these three elements is key to achieving well-exposed photographs.
- **Depth of Field:** The range of distance that appears acceptably sharp in an image. A

shallow depth of field (achieved with a wider aperture) isolates the subject from the background, while a deep depth of field (achieved with a smaller aperture) keeps more of the scene in focus.

- **RAW:** A high-quality image file format that retains all the data from the camera's sensor. RAW files offer more flexibility for post-processing compared to JPEGs, as they contain more detail and information.
- **White Balance (WB):** The adjustment of colors in an image to ensure that whites appear neutral and accurate under different light conditions. Proper white balance prevents color casts (e.g., too blue or too orange).
- **Focus Peaking:** A feature that highlights in-focus areas when using manual focus, making it easier to achieve sharp focus, especially in macro photography or video.
- **Burst Mode:** A setting that allows the camera to take multiple shots in quick succession, useful for action photography or when capturing fast-moving subjects.
- **Bokeh:** The aesthetic quality of the out-of-focus areas in an image, typically created by a wide aperture. Bokeh can help make the subject stand out by blurring distracting backgrounds.
- **EVF (Electronic Viewfinder):** The viewfinder on mirrorless cameras like the Nikon Z5II, which displays the image digitally. EVFs allow you to see the

exposure, focus, and other settings before taking the shot.

- **Metering Mode:** The method the camera uses to calculate exposure. The Nikon Z5II offers multiple metering modes such as Matrix, Center-weighted, and Spot metering to suit different lighting conditions.

Nikon Z5II Full Technical Specifications

Here's an overview of the key features and specifications of the Nikon Z5II:

- **Sensor Type:** Full-frame (35.9 x 23.9mm) CMOS sensor
- **Image Processor:** EXPEED 6
- **ISO Range:** 100-51,200 (expandable to 50–204,800)
- **Autofocus:** Hybrid AF system with 273 phase-detection points and Eye Detection
- **Continuous Shooting Speed:** Up to 4.5 frames per second
- **Viewfinder:** 3.69 million-dot OLED electronic viewfinder
- **Display:** 3.2-inch, 1.04 million-dot LCD touchscreen
- **Video:** 4K UHD at 30p, 1080p at 120p (Full HD)
- **Connectivity:** Wi-Fi, Bluetooth, USB-C, HDMI output

- **Battery Life:** Approximately 470 shots (CIPA rating)
- **Dual SD Card Slots:** Supports UHS-II SD cards for faster write speeds
- **Weather Sealing:** Yes, designed to withstand moisture and dust
- **Size and Weight:** 134 x 101 x 60 mm (5.28 x 3.98 x 2.36 inches), weighs about 650g (1.43 lbs)
- **Other Features:**
  - 5-axis in-body image stabilization (IBIS)
  - 4K UHD recording with full pixel readout
  - 14-bit RAW output for professional-grade post-processing
  - 273-point hybrid autofocus system (including eye detection)
  - Dual card slots for flexible storage options
  - 10-bit HDMI output for enhanced video quality
  - 1.5x crop for 4K video shooting

How to Contact Nikon Support and Service Centers

In case you need assistance or repairs for your Nikon Z5II, here's how to get in touch with Nikon Support:

1. Phone Support (U.S.):

- **Nikon USA Contact Number:** 1-800-NIKON-UX (1-800-645-6686)
- Available Monday to Friday from 9 AM to 8 PM (Eastern Time)

2. Email Support:

- Visit Nikon's support page to submit a support request or find email options for your country or region.

3. Live Chat:

- Nikon offers live chat support during business hours. You can access this service via the support page on the Nikon website.

4. Service Centers:

- For repairs or servicing, use the **Service Locator** on Nikon's official website to find authorized repair centers near you. Visit Nikon Service Locator.

5. Warranty Information:

- Nikon provides a limited warranty for its cameras and lenses. You can check warranty details and register your product for warranty purposes on the Nikon website.

By reaching out to Nikon support or visiting an authorized service center, you ensure your Nikon Z5II stays in top condition throughout its lifespan.

www.ingramcontent.com/pod-product-compliance
Lightning Source LLC
LaVergne TN
LVHW022350060326
832902LV00022B/4365